O WHO WILL MARRY ME?

O who will marry me?

A Book of Country Love

Ralph Whitlock

EX LIBRIS PRESS

Published in 1995 by
EX LIBRIS PRESS
1 The Shambles
Bradford on Avon
Wiltshire
BA15 1JS

Design and typesetting by
Ex Libris Press

Cover printed by
Shires Press, Trowbridge, Wiltshire
Printed in Britain by
Cromwell Press, Broughton Gifford, Wiltshire

ISBN 0 948578 71 8

Like its sister volume, *March Winds and April Showers* (Ex Libris Press 1993), this book is illustrated throughout with engravings by Thomas Bewick, 1753-95. Thankyou, once again, Thomas. The illustrations are taken from *1800 Woodcuts by Thomas Bewick and his School* (Dover Publications, 1962)

Contents

Introduction 7

LOVE LORE 9

THE CHRISTMAS SEASON 21

ST. VALENTINE'S DAY 29

MAY DAY AND MIDSUMMER 35

HARVESTS AND AUTUMN FAIRS 47

HALLOWE'EN 55

CHRISTMAS AND THE FIRST-FOOTER 65

O, WHO WILL MARRY ME? 73

INTRODUCTION

'O who will marry me?' The question, half-jocular, was tinged with anxiety. For a girl to reach the age of twenty with no prospects of marriage was a highly undesirable state of affairs.

In the higher ranks of society the question was academic. The girl married whom she was told to. A king's daughter was a considerable asset to her father, to be bestowed on someone of equal status. It was just too bad if her suitor was old enough to be her grandfather. She must have often prayed that the arranged marriage would be at least with someone of the right age, though often it wasn't.

Lower in the social scale the same rules applied. Here again the girl, especially if an heiress, was a family asset, to be disposed of to the best advantage. A certain amount of latitude could be allowed to a daughter who had several older brothers, but she was not expected to marry out of her class.

For a girl of the proletariat the rules were rather different. She could hardly marry beneath her. And what were the alternatives to marriage?

She could stay at home to help her mother with the rearing of a large family: a prospect which entailed a great deal of hard work for very little reward. Or she could take employment at some big house in the neighbourhood, often on a village farm. She could get a job at a factory or mill. After the coming of the railways there was a strong demand for village girls in the upper-class houses of London and other large towns. But there was no professional employment and wages or salaries were low. No careers were open to a village or city girl. And if she lost her job and had to retire to the family home for a time, her father soon got tired of supporting an unproductive member of the family. "When in the world is our Agnes going to get married?" he would ask.

Marriage, then, was the only escape from near-slavery. It was a chancy business. There was no guarantee of success. But to some extent a married woman was mistress of her own destiny. She had her own home, and her life in it depended to some extent on her skill in managing her husband. And a married woman had in her community a status denied to her unmarried sister.

So, by and large, it was the ambition of every girl to achieve that status, to get married. And as the years passed, there came an increased urgency into the question, Who will marry me? And they devised a multifarious collection of signs, portents, omens and divinations to aid them in getting an answer.

Appealing to the New Moon

According to John Aubrey, the seventeenth century antiquary, English girls would appeal to the new moon by reciting the following rhyme:

All haile to thee, moon, all hail to thee,
I prithee, good moon, declare to me
This night, who my husband must be.

'This they do,' Aubrey adds, 'sitting astride on a gate or a stile, the first evening the new moon appears.'

The Waxing Moon

For a successful marriage it should be celebrated when the moon is waxing.

The New Moon and the Saints

The first new moon in January must be seen by a girl, alone, and looking over a gate. She must then offer prayers on St. Agnes' Eve (January 20th), which, if answered, would cause her true love to appear to her in a dream.

An associated item of lore was to gather May dew at daybreak on May Day. There is a rhyme which runs:

Maid who on the first of May
Goeth afield at break of day;
Wash thy face in dew off the hawthorn tree
And for ever after a fair maid shall be.

Yarrow to encourage Love

Yarrow was held to encourage love in the heart of a shy young man. A girl had to pin a bunch of the flowers on her dress and take every opportunity to get as close as possible to the young man of her choice and to make sure that he noticed the flowers. If he ignored the sign she must persevere. At the time of the next full moon she should go at midnight and walk barefoot through a patch of yarrow. Then she must shut her eyes and, bending down, pick a bunch of the flowers and put them under her bed. If at dawn the flowers were still wet with dew, all would be well. She could expect the romance to develop.

On the other hand, if the flowers were dry there was no need to despair. The ritual could be repeated at the time of the next full moon!

Artemisia as a token

Artemisia, or Southernwood, was used by bashful young men in the Fens as a signal to girls that he was interested. Before setting out for a walk on a summer evening he would cut some sprigs of the plant and stick them in his buttonhole. After a time he would encounter a group of girls, whom he would pass, ostentatiously sniffing at his buttonhole. If the girls turned round and came back towards him, he would remove the plant and hand it to the girl of his choice. After a show of reluctance she would pin it to her dress and, linking her arm with his, go off on their first courting stroll.

A True-lover's Knot

Another Fenland custom was more formal and involved confronting the girl in the presence of her parents after church on a Sunday evening. The young man would make two tokens, each of three ears of wheat tied together with straw to make a true-lover's knot. One of these he would pin on his Sunday smock, on the right side of his chest but with the ears of wheat inclining to the left. On leaving church he handed the second one to the girl, without uttering a word.

On reaching home, she placed the token before her parents, and a family conference followed, as to the suitability or otherwise of the young man. He had to wait till the next Sunday for his answer. If it was pinned over her heart, with the ears of wheat pointing to the right, all was well. He was accepted. But if she wore the token on the right side of her dress, the family did not approve of him as a future son-in-law.

The lover's knots were preserved, in a place of honour in the future home and were admired in due course by grandchildren.

The Glastonbury Thorn and a Rose at Christmas.

At Glastonbury, in Somerset, there is a thorn tree, reputed to be descended from one which sprang up from a rod carried by Joseph of Arimathea when he landed at Glastonbury as a refugee from Palestine at a time of persecution. This thorn tree is supposed to bloom every year on Christmas Day. In 1752, when the calendar was changed, Old Christmas Day fell on January 5th, 1753, and a great crowd of people gathered on the two relevant dates to see on which one the thorn would bloom. As a matter of fact, that year it is said to have bloomed on January 5th.

For many years before and after that date many people used to gather at Glastonbury to see the Thorn bloom. The country folk would break off twigs of blossom at midnight and use them for divination, including as a love potion.

If a West Country girl has doubts about whether her lover is true to her, she has only to pick a rose on Midsummer Day. It will remain fresh until Christmas Day, and if she will then wear it in her bosom to church on that day he will come and take it from her. It seems a long time to wait for fulfilment of a promise.

Divination from Plants

The Ashen Faggot: At Christmas-time an old custom was to burn an ashen faggot on the hearth. A large faggot of green ash stlcks,tightly bound with rods of ash and hazel, was burned in the presence of a family party at Christmas. All the young people of marriageable age were invited to choose one of the encircling bands, and the owner of the first band to break in the fire would be the first to get married. Almost needless to say, the breaking of the band is a signal to the drinking of a cider toast to the happy couple.

Peeling an Apple: For a girl to discover the identity of her future husband she had to peel an apple, keeping the peel whole and intact, and throw it over her left shoulder. Examination of the peel would reveal that it had fallen in the shape of a letter (though sometimes somewhat fanciful), and this would be the initial of the future bridegroom.

Counting Daisies: To learn the identity of her future husband, a girl had to pick a bunch of daisies with her eyes shut. The number of flowers she picked represented the number of years she would have to wait.

Sowing Hemp Seed: A girl really anxious to know the identity of her future husband had to walk alone from the church porch to her home at half-an-hour after midnight on Saint Valentine's Day. As she walked she had to scatter hemp seed and to recite a spell. Then, looking over her shoulder, she would see the ghost of her future husband following behind and raking it into a winding-sheet.

According to another version girls (and boys) went together as a party and sang the following ditty as they walked:

Hempseed I sow; hempseed I sow;
He/she that will my true love be
Come, rake this hemp seed after me.

Hempseed, incidentally, is better known nowadays as cannabis.

Ode to a Clover Leaf

If you wish to know the name of your future husband, put a two-leaved clover into your right shoe and recite:

A clover of two, a clover of two,
Put it in your right shoe;
The first young man you meet
In field, street or lane,
You'll have him or one of his name.

Rosemary for Dominance: If a girl seeks to be the dominant partner in her marriage she should plant rosemary in her garden.

Valerian for Love: To encourage thoughts of love in your partner make sure you have some valerian in your pocket.

Vervain when you are courting: An engaged couple should exchange leaves of a vervain plant and keep them carefully in their Bibles. If the leaves remained green, then their love would prosper; but if they turned brown it was a sign that love was fading.

A vervain leaf sent to a lover
Carries a message; you need no other.

Divination by means of onions: A writer in the early eighteenth century quotes the following rhyme which he says he often heard in country districts:

In those same days young wanton gyrles that mete for marriage be
Do serche to know the names of those that shall their husbands be,
Four onyons, five or eight they take, and make to everyeone
Such names as the doe fancie most and best to think upon.
Then near the chimney them they set, and that same onyon, then
That first doe sprout doth surely bear the name of their good man.

Divination by the cuckoo's calls: When a girl hears the first cuckoo of the spring she kisses her hands and repeats, "Cuckoo, cuckoo, when shall I be married." The number of times the cuckoo calls indicates the number of years she will have to wait.

Alternatively, when a group of girls heard the first cuckoo they immediately started to run, and ran as fast as they could until they could go no farther. They then sat down and took off the boots from their left foot. At the bottom of the boot they would find a hair the exact colour of the hair of the boy they would marry.

At the other end of life an old dame, beset with infirmities, would, on hearing the cuckoo, ask, "Cuckoo, cuckoo,when shall I be released from this world's cares?" Again the answer came in the number of calls the cuckoo made. A comment, often repeated, was that the poor bird was kept so busy answering all these question that it never had time to build a nest of her own and so was forced to lay her eggs in another bird's nest!

When you hear the first cuckoo, if the call comes from the right the coming year will bring for you prosperity; but if from the left you will have bad luck.

Divination by means of Dumb Cake: St. Mark's Day is April 25th, and certain popular superstitions were attached to St. Mark's Eve. The one which most concerns us was for not more than three women to combine to make a Dumb Cake. They had to do it in complete silence. Then, after it had been baked, at twelve o'clock midnight, each broke off a piece of the cake and ate it. They then had to walk backwards to their bedroom. Those who were to be married in the coming year would hear a man's footsteps approaching, but those who would remain unmarried heard nothing.

Another St. Mark's Eve custom was for a girl to pluck three tufts of grass from a churchyard. Before they went to sleep they had to repeat aloud:

Let me know my fate, whether weal or woe;
Whether my rank's to be high or low;
Whether to live single or be a bride,
And the destiny my star doth provide.

She would then dream of her future fate.

An alternatlve version of the Dumb Cake required the girl to fast for several hours and then to sit alone and make the cake in complete silence. Into the cake she had to put an egg-shell-full of salt and an equal quantity of wheat meal and barley meal. Her reward was the sight of her future husband at midnight, if she opened the door just after turning the cake.

A trio of divination aids were of use only in country villages which held only one practitioner of a specialist trade or profession, such as a blacksmlth, a tailor or a bricklayer. Again on St. Mark's Eve, to discover the identity of her true love a girl had to set two pewter pots on a freshly whitened hearthstone and silently go to bed, walking backwards. When looking under the pots the next morning she would find something that would give her a clue to her future partner's occupation. An example would be a piece of wood if he were a carpenter, a thread if he were a tailor or a sprinkling of soil if he worked on the land.

Alternatively, if the first egg laid by a hen in spring was

broken into a glass and left standing overnight the yolk would have assumed a shape which would give her a clue as to how he earned his daily bread.

More dramatic was the requirement that, after dark, she were to dig a hole at the cross-roads and apply her ear to it she would hear a sound which would indicate his trade or profession.

Incidentally, a more sinister superstition associated with St. Mark's Eve was to keep a vigil, fasting, at the church door just before midnight. As the church clock struck twelve the watcher would see the spirits of those parishioners doomed to die in the coming year walking into the church.

To our rural ancestors certain seasons were held to be especially conducive to thoughts of love and marriage. Chief among them were Christmas and the New Year; St.Valentine's Day; Easter and Palm Sunday; May Day and Whitsuntide; Haymaking and Sheep-shearing; Harvest Home; Hallowe'en.

FIRST LOVE

I ne'er was struck before that hour
  With love so sudden and so sweet,
Her face it bloomed like a sweet flower
  And stole my heart away complete.

My face turned pale as deadly pale,
  My legs refused to walk away,
And when she looked, what could I ail?
  My life and all seemed turned to clay.

And then my blood rushed to my face
  And took my eyesight quite away,
The trees and bushes round the place
  Seemed midnight at noonday.
I could not see a single thing,
  Words from my eyes did start –
They spoke as chords do from the string,
  And blood burnt round my heart.

Are flowers the winter's choice?
  Is love's bed always snow?
She seemed to hear my silent voice,
  Not love's appeals to know.
I never saw so sweet a face
  As that I stood before.
My heart has left its dwelling-place
  And can return no more.

JOHN CLARE (1793-1864)

We have already mentioned the burning of the ashen faggot on the hearth at Christmas. The faggot is fastened by bonds of withy, and as it burns the first bond to snap is an indication that whoever had chosen it would be the first to get married.

A girl must never on Christmas Eve sleep on a bed unadorned by a spray of holly. If she remembers so to decorate her bed she will dream of her true love, but if she neglects to do so she will be troubled by nightmares. But she has no excuse, for it is considered unlucky to start putting up Christmas decorations before Christmas Eve, and so that day is spent busily in decorating the house.

There is an old belief that a mince-pie eaten in a different house on the Twelve Days of Christmas will ensure twelve lucky months. Testing this belief, parties of young men and girls used to spend the twelve days visiting the houses of their friends and neighbours and sampling the mince-pies of the house. In Somerset, girls used to make a special sort of bun, known as a 'simlin,' for the occasion, and certain divinations were attached to the eating of them, but these have been forgotten.

The custom attached to the 'first-footer' is still observed in some places. The first person to enter a house on New Year's Day should be tall, dark and handsome and should bring with him gifts of food, drink and fuel. In some versions there is an emphasis on a token gift of money. The underlying idea is to bring luck to the household and ensure that during the coming year it shall not lack bread, ale or wood or the cash to buy it. Variations in the requirements included that the first-footer must not have a squint or be lame. In other districts there was a prejudice against a red-haired man (doubtless a distant memory of the Danish pirates), and on no account must the first-footer be a woman.

Another belief is that on New Year's Day a person should leave the house empty-handed and return heavily-laden ... thus ensuring that during the coming year he will receive more than he will give away. It is also considered that the first water drawn from a well on New Year's Day has the property of giving beauty and good luck. Where this is still credited there is considerable competition among girls to be first at the well after midnight!

A Christmas tradition in Devon was for a girl to visit a hen-house at night and quietly open it. If the cock crowed she would marry before the end of the coming year; but if the hens started cackling, she would never marry! Or she could go to the wood-pile after dark and bring back an armful of logs to the house without counting them. If when she counted them the next morning there proved to be an even number she would marry in the coming year; otherwise she would have to wait longer.

A custom belonging to St. Thomas's Day (December 20th) was for an unmarried girl to peel a large onion at bedtime and stick nine pins into it. Then she had to chant:

> *Good St.Thomas, do me right,*
> *Send me my true love tonight.*

She was more likely to be disappointed, except in dreams.

It is lucky to give away money and food on New Year's Day, and a child who is born on January 1st will bring good luck to all the family. But a housewife who sweeps her house before sunrise on New Year's morning will invite bad luck.

To avoid being bewitched during the coming year, tie the garter of your left leg in two bows on January 1st.

Because each line of the following very old song begins with,

my true love sent to me ...

it must have something to do with love and courtship, but readers must puzzle over what it means:

On the first day of Christmas my true love sent to me,
a part of a juniper tree;
On the second day of Christmas my true love sent to me,
two turtle doves and a part of a juniper tree;
On the third day of Christmas my true love sent to me,
three French hens, two turtles doves and a part of a juniper tree, etc ...
On the fourth day of Christmas my true love sent to me,
four collie birds, three French hens, etc ...
On the fifth day of Christmas my true love sent to me ,
five golden rings, four collie birds, etc ...
On the sixth day of Christmas my true love sent to me,
six geese a-laying, five golden rings, etc ...
On the seventh day of Christmas my true love sent to me,
seven swans a-swimming, six geese a-laying, etc.
On the eighth day of Christmas my true love sent to me,
eight hares a-running, seven swans a-swimming, etc
On the ninth day of Christmas my true love sent to me,
nine bears a-biting, eight hares a-running. etc ...
On the tenth day of Christmas my true love sent to me,
ten ladies a-dancing, nine bears a-biting, etc ...
On the eleventh day of Christmas my true love sent to me, eleven lords a-leaping, ten ladies a-dancing, etc...
On the twelfth day of Christmas my true love sent to me,
twelve bulls a-blaring, eleven lords a-leaping, etc ...

In Scotland Hogmanay, the last day of the old year, was traditionally celebrated by parties at which everyone stayed up till the clock struck twelve. Then they all wished each other a Happy New Year and exchanged kisses under the mistletoe. Doubtless the younger members of the party made the most of the opportunity.

In general the use of mistletoe in decorating churches at Christmas was frowned upon, though it sometimes found its way in with other evergreens, until a parson noticed it and had it removed. It came into its own, however, in the kitchen, where it was hung up it great state with its white berries; and when a female chanced to stand under it a young man observing it could claim the right of saluting her with an ardent kiss and of plucking off a berry at each kiss. It was held that a girl not kissed under the mistletoe at Christmas would not be married during the coming year.

A variation in the customs associated with the Dumb Cake (see page 11) comes from the Cotswolds. The ritual was carried out on Christmas Eve, rather than on St. Mark's eve, and the cake must be made by the girl alone. She had, however, to work in complete silence and when she had finished it and set it to bake she must prick her initials on it. At midnight, as she kept watch, her future husband would come into the room and prick his initials on the cake beside hers. She then had to eat the cake.

A widespread feature of the Feast of Twelfth-tide was the baking of a splendid cake, the most important ingredient of which was a bean and a pea. Everyone present at the meal eagerly searched their slice for the elusive bean and pea. The man who found it was forthwith crowned King of the Bean and presided over the revels for their duration. Likewise the girl who found the pea became Queen of the Pea. Which was as good a way as any of pairing off a couple.

In the Scottish Highlands the Christmas cheese, an important item in the Christmas feasts, was supposed to be strong magic. Anyone who lost his way on the hills had only to look through a hole in a slice of this cheese to find his way home. Girls used the same device to discover the identity of their future husband, though the details of the process have been lost.

Reverting to the first-footer, it was considered very unlucky for the first visitor to be a woman, and, indeed, it was bad luck for any woman who had not slept in the house to enter it on New Year's Day before noon, no matter how many men had preceded her.

There was a strong belief in Wales and the Welsh border counties that the first water drawn from a well on

New Year's Day had magical qualities. Girls would stay up on New Year's Eve and race to be first to draw water from the well after midnight. The water not only brought them good luck but also enhanced their attractions in the eyes of the lads.

LOUISA

After accompanying her on
a mountain excursion

I met Louisa in the shade,
And, having seen that lovely Maid,
Why should I fear to say
That, nymph-like, she is fleet and strong.
And down the rocks can leap along
Like rivulets in May?

And she hath smiles to earth unknown;
Smiles, that with motion of their own
Do spread, and sink, and rise;
That come and go with endless play,
And ever, as they pass away,
Are hidden in her eyes.

She loves her fire, her cottage-home;
Yet o'er the moorland will she roam
In weather rough and bleak;
And, when against the wind she strains,
Oh! might I kiss the mountain rains
That sparkle on her cheek.

Take all that's mine 'beneath the moon,'
If I with her but half a noon
May sit beneath the walls
Of some old cave, or mossy nook,
When up she winds along the brook
To hunt the waterfalls.

WILLIAM WORDSWORTH (1770-1850)

St. Valentine's Day

St.Valentine's Day, February 14th, would seem to be an unlikely date of interest to young lovers, but it happens to be the eve of the Roman festival of Lupercalia – a festival of youth – to which it owes far more than to the saintly Valentine. St.Valentine was, as a matter of fact, renowned for his chastity. February 14th was also the day by which birds chose their mates, which seemed a convenient example for humans to follow.

A traditional procedure was by drawing lots. In its simplest form you wrote your name on a piece of paper which was placed in a hat or a vase. Then everyone present drew a slip of paper until all had become some-one's Valentine. Another tradition despatched with even this formula. It assumed that the first person of the opposite sex seen on the morning of St. Valentine's Day automatically became your Valentine.

Wide credence used to be attached to the counting of fruit stones around one's plate. What will be the occupation of your sweetheart?

Tinker, tailor, soldier, sailor, rich man,
poor man, beggar-man, thief.

When will you be married?
This year, next year, sometime, never.

Of what material will be my bridal gown?
Silk, satin, muslin, rags.

The world of Nature was accorded a wider importance than it would be today. For instance, if a girl found an ash-leaf with an even number of segments she would recite,

This even-ash I hold in my hand –
the first I meet is my true man.

However, there was an escape clause. She would ask the name of the first man she met, but if she didn't like the look of him she would look for someone with the same name. The same procedure could be followed with a four-leaf clover, but before chanting the spell the clover had to be hidden in the right shoe.

Unmarried girls would, in the Fens, wear their stockings inside out, to ensure of getting a husband before the rising of the Harvest Moon.

The sending of Valentine cards enjoyed enormous popularity in Victorian times and has recently become fashionable again. Not many girls, however, will know the language of flowers, which was part of the lore of Victorian damsels. Here are some of the most important.

Almond blossom expressed hope and is a symbol of delicacy.
Anemone flowers – soon fade.
Bachelor's button, or *cornflower* – as long as it remained fresh so would love. But inevitably it faded.
Buttercup – the flower of childhood. But as childhood fades so does gratitude.
Carnation – a symbol of marriage and eternal love. But an older tradition associated it with the grave of true love.
Columbine – alas, for a deserted lover.
Chrysanthemum – the flower of love, if it is red. But if it is yellow it speaks of thwarted love; and if white, of truth, even if not entirely pleasant.
Daffodil – the flower of death and deceit.
Forget-me-not – the flower of true love.
Hyacinth – excellence in sport or play. In ancient Greece it was used in bridal wreaths.
Lily – usually regarded as a symbol of purity. But it was also considered an unlucky flower and spoke of falsehood or treachery.
Periwinkle – the flower of friendship and pleasant memories. But an older tradition remembers that it was woven into crowns worn by criminals on their way to execution.
Poppy – If you take the petal of a poppy in your palm and hit it with your fist it will make a snapping sound, that is, if you can trust your love to be faithful. A red poppy is for consolation, if he isn't.
Rose – Of all flowers, this is the one most wholeheartedly dedicated to love. But a yellow rose is a symbol of jealousy.

Snowdrop – Indicates consolation, and hope.
Sunflower – As a symbol of the sun, it stands for haughtiness.
Tulip – Another symbol of love, and of passionate love at that. But a yellow tulip stands for hopeless love.

Snowdrops in the Welsh border shires are known as Christ's Flowers, or, alternatively, as Candlemas Bells, Purification Flowers or Fair Maid of February. In some places it was a tradition to bring a bunch of snowdrops into the hourse on Candlemas Day, though at other times it was considered unlucky.

In Cornwall the first man seen by a girl on St. Valentine's Day would be her husband – or a man of the same name. A Cornish verse offers some valuable advice to young men contemplating marriage:

Come all you young men with your wicked ways,
Sow all your wild oats in your youthful days,
That we may live happy, that we may live happy,
That we may live happy when we grow old.

And the practicalities of married life were not forgotten in the rhyme:

O proper maid, if you'll be mine,
Send me back some binder twine!

There is a record of an interesting custom observed in Hertfordshire until about the middle of last century. All the youngsters of the parish gathered together and marched to the house of the most prominent citizen.

Wreaths and true-lover's knots were thrown from the windows, and the youngsters adorn themselves with these. Then they paraded around the town or village, collecting pence and regaling the listeners with a song:

Good morrow to you, Valentine,
Curl your locks as I do mine,
Two before and three behind,
Good morrow to you, Valentine.

This, however, is a children's custom and has the motive of soliciting pence from the populace.

Naturally, St. Valentine's Day was a popular occasion for announcing an engagment, and for collecting appropriate presents. Valentine cards and bouquets of flowers were among the favourite, but Enid Porter, in *Cambridgeshire Customs and Folklore*, records an interesting example in which the man caused a Valentine gift to be sent to his sweetheart at hourly intervals throughout the day, culminating in a gold watch at six o'clock in the evening.

Generally, however,a Valentine pairing was taken light-heartedly. At parties the couples were often paired off by lot. It was also an occasion for leaving gifts surreptitiously on doorsteps and inviting the recipients to guess who sent them. In the days before Valentine cards became popular a pair of gloves was considered to be an appropriate Valentine gift.

If, on the morning of Valentine's Day, a single girl met an eligible young man she could expect to be married within three months, but if her first encounter was with another woman she wouldn't be married that year.

ECHO

Come to me in the silence of the night;
  Come in the speaking silence of a dream;
Come with soft rounded cheeks and eyes as bright
  As sunlight on a stream;
    Come back in tears,
O memory, hope, love of finished years.

O dream how sweet, too sweet, too bitter sweet,
  Whose wakening should have been in Paradise,
Where souls brimfull of love abide and meet;
  Where thirsting longing eyes
    Watch the slow door
That opening, letting in, lets out no more.

Yet come to me in dreams, that I may live
  My very life again though cold in death:
Come back to me in dreams, that I may give
  Pulse for pulse, breath for breath:
    Speak low, lean low,
As long ago, my love, how long ago.

CHRISTINA ROSETTI (1830-94)

May Day and Midsummer

The Puritans, in the seventeenth century, were rightly suspicious of everything connected with May Day. They saw in it a licentious festival concerned with pagan fertility rites, as we can appreciate. In the May mornings the air is filled with bird song; the swallows have returned to their barn nests; bluebells, primroses, celandines and wood anemones are carpeting the woods. Newly-sown seed is sprouting. Newborn lambs are in the meadows, and newly-hatched chicks in the farmyards. Bees are laying the foundations of new swarms. Birds everywhere are mating and nesting. To our ancestors, closer to Nature than we are, everything around them spoke of fertility and growth. What could be more natural than for humans to feel the urge to join in?

So to the greenwoods the young men and girls went daily, eager to participate in the rites of the renewal of life. And in the morning they brought back with them green boughs, freshly bursting into life, as tokens that they had done just that. Virtually all May Day customs and traditions have that basis.

A song has been running through my head recently. We used to sing it as a round in the village school I attended, seventy years ago:

May Day's breaking; all the world's awaking;
Let me see the sun rise over the Plain.
Why have you awoke me? How you do provoke me!
Let me have a little time to doze off again.
Sleeping in the daytime, wastes the happy Maytime,
Makes an empty pocket and a cloudy brain.

I am puzzled to know whether this is a genuine folk song of great antiquity or simply some edifying verses composed in Victoria's reign. The reference to the 'Plain' is suggestive, for if Salisbury Plain is meant, the line about seeing the sun rise would seem to refer to Stonehenge, where crowds still gather to see the sun rise on the summer solstice.

Some of the May Day customs have changed their date. One May Day morning I got up at about half-past two and climbed to the top of Cerne Abbas Hill and, looking down on the great carving of the Giant, watched the Wessex Morris Dancers perform their traditional dance. And how welcome we found the piping hot breakfast we had waiting for us at the local inn.

On another occasion I climbed out of bed at about half-past three and went over to Wishford, only to find I was too late to trudge up the hill to Groveley Wood, to help gather green branches to decorate the church tower. As a matter of fact, that wasn't actually on May

Day, for Wishford is one of those villagers that have changed the date of its festival. It happened in the time of the Commonwealth, when Parliament, controlled by sober and strait-laced Puritans, even prohibited the observance of Christmas and Easter, let alone May Day. So all festivities were in abeyance, and when they were revived, on the restoration of Charles II, people had forgotten a lot of the details . Anyway, Oak Apple Day was King Charles' particular festival and most people were glad to have the Merry Monarch back.

The Wishford ceremony is one of considerable antiquity. The Sum of the Ancient Customs belonging to Wishford and Barford out of the Forest of Groveley is the title of a document prepared in the reign of Henry VIII. Besides confirming that the villagers may gather wood in the Forest, send cattle and pigs to graze there and to kill one fat buck there every Whitsuntide, the deed testifies to the antiquity, even at that date, of some of the associated customs. It states:

> The Lords, Freeholders, Tenants and Inhabitants of the Manor of Great Wishford, or so many of them as would, in ancient time have used to go in a dance to the Cathedral Church of Our Blessed Lady in the City of New Sarum on Whit Tuesday, in the said county of Wilts, and there they made their claim to the custom in the forest of Groveley in these words: Groveley! Groveley! Groveley! and all Groveley.

And so we undertook our pilgrimage to Salisbury and there before the High Altar of the Catheral raised our shout of Groveley! Groveley! and all Groveley!

The crowd assembled to watch the ceremony when last I was there was remarkably small, no doubt because this annual celebration is not widely known. The Wishford Oak Apple festival, of which this is part, is not organised with an eye to publicity, though the public is welcome to attend if they happen to hear about it. What goes on at Wishford is an artless and spontaneous participation in an age-old celebration for its own sake. Whether or not there are any spectators matters not at all to the villagers.

A similar pageant occurred in countless parishes throughout all England. The lads and girls who ventured into the woods before daybreak of May Day morning were ritually conveying the fertilising power of Nature to the community. As a token of what they had done they returned to their homes bearing flowers and green boughs for decoration.

As time passed the pageant in many parishes became crystallised into a play, with recognisable characters, chief of which were Robin Hood and Maid Marian. There was also the Green Man, or Jack-in-the-Green's character heavily disguised by greenery, who in the course of time merged with the Chimney Sweep. Maid Marian became the May Queen, who was duly crowned with much pageantry, and the festivities continued with dancing around the Maypole, which was traditionally a hawthorn tree. But beyond any doubt the maypole was originally a phallic symbol, and none of our ancestors had any doubt as to its significance.

So strong was its hold on popular sentiment that in the Puritan reaction of the seventeenth century it bred its own reaction. Chaucer records how in the fourteenth century everyone went forth into the woods and fields, 'to fetche the flowres fresh, and brounche and blome, fresh garlands of the hawthorne,' to decorate the maypole. In Suffolk it was an old custom that any servant who could bring in a branch of hawthorn in full bloom on May Day morning was entitled to a dish of cream for breakfast. But in Somerset, a stronghold of Puritanism, a tradition arose that on no account must Mayflower be brought into the house in May. To do so would invite ill-luck, accident and even death.

The month of May was considered an unlucky month, and especially for weddings.

Marry in May, and you'll rue the day.

Marry in May, and repent alway.

To wed in May is to wed poverty.

The proverbs teach, and common people say
It's ill to marry in the month of May.

A May chit (girl) is no good.

Marry in May and you'll marry a slattern.

All of which is in direct contrast with the former universal rejoicing which greeted May Day morning when to give an example of what went on at Minehead, 'all the people went to Whitecross, where a Maypole was erected and, to the music of clarionets, lasses and lads danced around the decorated pole and crowned, not only a queen, but also a King of the May. The children donned white aprons on May Day morning and went out into the fields to catch the dew, afterwards choosing from among the prettiest girls and making her Queen of the May.'

One would have thought that, in the face of all this festivity, May would have been the most popular month of the year for weddings, but not a bit of it. Incidentally, with so much liaising between the sexes in the woods on May Day, one might have expected to find a bumper crop of babies born in the following February, but I can detect not a trace of such an association.

There is, however, a very old tradition concerning May dew. It was said that if a lass went into the fields on May Day and washed her face in the dew, that would rid her complexion of freckles.

The fair maid who, the first of May,
Goes to the fields at break of day
And washes in dew from the hawthorn tree,
Will ever after handsome be.

Here again, an enigmatic reference to a hawthorn tree. Another belief was that anyone suffering from ill-health should get up early on May Day morning and lick the dew off the leaves of a hawthorn tree. May dew was also held to have curative properties, but to be effective it had to be gathered from the grave of the last young woman buried in the parish; or, if a man was the supplicant, of the last young man!

Despite the conspiracy of all Nature to encourage love-making in early summer, folklore is remarkably silent on the relationship between the sexes. Indeed, the next calendar date associated with courtship and love is Midsummer. Or, to be more precise, St. John's Eve, June 23rd. It is associated with the ancient custom of keeping vigil on that night, though young people were quick to take advantage of being out and about all through the short midsummer nights.

The more sober associations of the vigil were to determine who were the parishioners doomed to die in the coming year. Hardy characters could conceal themselves in the church porch and take note of the phantoms who entered the building. Those who came out again would suffer from an illness during the year but would recover. Those who did not re-emerge would assuredly die. It is said that a sexton who thus concealed himself did so in order to be able to calculate his annual income from grave-digging!

A girl who wished to know what the future held for her, however, lay the table for supper, open all the doors, and, concealed, wait till the clock strikes midnight. As she watches, a figure appears, eats the supper and vanishes. She then has to wait twelve hours, till the following mid-day. Then, after having borrowed a wedding-ring, she has to tie it to one of her hairs and suspend it over a glass of water. She has to time it very carefully, for while the clock is striking twelve she has to be counting the number of times the ring tinkles against the glass. And that number will be the number of years that must elapse before she becomes a wife.

A process which must lend itself to considerable temptation is for her to place under her bed a basin filled with water. In it she places a number of cardboard letters of the alphabet. Next morning she inspects them and finds that a number of them have turned over. Properly arranged, they prove to be the initial letters of her husband-to-be. But it must be a girl of remarkable probity who can resist giving the letters a little help.

The flower, Orpine, was widely regarded as a divinatory token. A bunch of these flowers, also known as Midsummer Men, was set on the hearth overnight. In the morning the anxious girl hurried down to consult them. If the stalks had turned to the right, her lover would be true to her; if to the left, he would prove false. This item of divinatory lore used to be widely practised in the West Country.

A girl very much in love would go alone and fill a cup with running water, while reciting:

Water, water, running free,
May my love run swift to me.

She then has to gather a bunch of red and white roses and arrange them in heart-shape on a table before an open window. In the morning she reads her fate in the condition of the roses. If they are still fresh, her lover will be true to her. If faded,the romance will cool. But if they are disarranged the girl herself will find another sweet-heart.

To take the process one step farther, she must shut her eyes and take a rose at random. If she has picked a red one, she will marry a rich man; if white, a poor one.

The laying of a clean white tablecloth on a table before an open door or window has an interesting variation. On the cloth lay a dish with a shoulder of lamb on it, and thoughtfully leave an open pen-knife handy. On the stroke of midnight a man will enter, stick the knife into the meat and walk away with it. This, however, would seem to require some pre-arrangement.

Here is a simple test which can hardly fail, provided the young man is forewarned. Boil an egg hard and, walking backwards, take it upstairs in a glass of water. Place it on a chair or table and get into bed backwards, saying:

It's not this egg I mean to eat,
But my true love's heart I mean to seek.
In his apparel and array
As he wears it every day.

Again, as the midnight hour strikes, the young man will appear and drink the water.

St. John's-wort is a golden flower in bloom at midsummer and so features quite prominently in our collection of charms. Properly used, it is gathered on Midsummer Eve and taken to the church porch where, well concealed, a girl may see her true love walk into the church. Many girls, however, are content to place a bunch of the flower under her pillow before she goes to sleep, believing that in her dreams she will see her true love.

An echo of the belief that a rose picked on Midsummer Day will remain fresh till Christmas is to be found in the tradition that if such a rose is worn to church on Christmas Day a girl's sweetheart will come and take it from her breast and put it in his buttonhole. Such an action will show that the young man can be trusted implicitly.

There is particularly potent magic in fern seed, which, a rarity in itself, must be gathered only at midnight on Midsummer Eve. It enabled the gatherer to find hidden treasure and to command any animal or bird to do his will, but its collection was dangerous and could produce madness.

Leaping through the flames of a bonfire on Midsummer Eve was widespread in the nineteenth century and was accompanied by dancing and merriment which continued on Orkney through the short night. At dawn, girls would retrieve a lump of partly burned peat and take it home with them. They extinguished the brand in the tub of urine which stood outside the crofter's door, and in the morning they broke it into two pieces. Examining the fibre which held the two pieces of peat together, they tried to match its colour with the colour of the hair of their future husband.

A similar tradition belonged to the Scottish Highlands on May Day. All fires in the houses were extinguished, to be relit from a central fire kindled on the moors. In this fire a large cake was baked and distributed among all the participants. One piece was daubed with charcoal and made quite black. Then all the men, blindfolded, queued up to select a piece from a receptacle. The man who drew the black slice was duly rewarded by favours from the girls, but in former times it was accepted as a sign that he was to be sacrificed.

TO MARY: I SLEEP WITH THEE, AND WAKE WITH THEE

I sleep with thee, and wake with thee,
  And yet thou art not there;
I fill my arms with thoughts of thee,
  And press the common air.
Thy eyes are gazing upon mine,
  When thou art out of sight;
My lips are always touching thine,
  At morning, noon, and night.

I think and speak of other things
  To keep my mind at rest:
But still to thee my memory clings
  Like love in woman's breast.
I hide it from the world's wide eye,
  And think and speak contrary;
But soft the wind comes from the sky,
  And whispers tales of Mary.

The night wind whispers in my ear,
  The moon shines in my face;
A burden still of chilling fear
  I find in every place.
The breeze is whispering in the bush,
  And the dews fall from the tree,
All sighing on, and will not hush,
  Some pleasant tales of thee.

JOHN CLARE (1793-1864)

The months of June, July and August are strangely lacking in the folklore of love, and that strikes me as being all the more remarkable because the summer months offer the maximum opportunities for courtship and flirtation. I speak from experience, having spent my teenage years helping with the haymaking, sheep-shearing, harvest and other farm activities which, mixing as they do the sexes in almost every phase of work-day experience, would seem to offer every chance for such carryings-on. Maybe there was sufficient incentive for a girl to be out of sight of a parental eye.

There are a few well-known tests of love to which an eager maiden can subscribe. If at daybreak on July 5th she will go into the garden and pick a crimson rose, she must keep it until bedtime and then put it under her pillow. Before going to sleep she must repeat the rhyme:

In my dreams I hope to see
The lad who is to marry me.

Then in her dreams she will see her future husband.

A 'true-lovers knot' is a favourite device to illustrate true love. It is now usually composed of colourful bunches of ribbons, arranged in the form of a knot, lightly stitched, and these would be stolen by young men at weddings. More accurately, a lovers' knot is made of three ears of wheat tied together with straw. For a couple to exchange this as a gift was a sign to their family that they were in earnest.

Girls' buttonholes had to be of yarrow. On their Sunday evening parade they would pin bunches of the flowers to their dresses and walk suggestively past the boys. If they ignored the hint a girl in earnest would wait for the next full moon and, at midnight, walk barefoot through a patch of yarrow. Then, shutting her eyes, she had to stoop down and pick a bunch of the flowers. Arriving home, she put the flowers under her bed or in a drawer and leave them till the morning. If the yarrow was still covered with dew it was a sign that the young man she had her eye on would be willing. But it was a bad sign if the flowers were dry; better to try again at the next full moon.

It was widely believed that if the harvest moon shone on the bed of a newly-married couple they would have a long and happy married life. But if a thunderstorm occurred during the wedding ceremony the marriage would be childless. It was always lucky for a couple to meet a sweep at the church door, and a thoughtful bridegroom would bribe the local sweep with a shilling and a gallon of beer.

As soon as possible after the wedding a wise bride would embroider a cross on her new husband's wedding smock. This was then wrapped in paper and stowed away in a chest, to be retrieved and buried with him if he happened to die first. The mother of a girl engaged to be married would look for a candle flame dividing into two as it burned. If she did, she would hurry on the arrangements for the wedding.

A rhyme from Cornwall offers some very sensible advice for the courtship period:

Come all you young men, with your wicked ways,
Sow all you in your youthful days,
That we may live happy, that we may live happy,
That we may live happy, when we grow old.

And from the same county a truly practical request from a young man to his girl friend:

O proper maid, if you'll be mine,
Please send me back some binder-twine.

The long days of summer offered ample opportunity for young men and girls to work on their own romances without bothering too much about signs and tokens. Here is an eyewitness account of the carrying-ons at a Cambridgeshire fair in the 1860s: 'Shoals of people everywhere about, and the heat was intense; the dancing booths were crammed full, pugilism was in the air, fighting was going on in all directions, in close proximity to love-making ... There was a babel of noise from the harp and violins, the blowing of horns and concertina playing. The whole pandemonium was punctuated by the noise of the skittle alley, a pastime much in vogue then.'

Many of the summer and autumn fairs were 'mop-fairs', or hiring fairs. Here men and women seeking for work for the coming year would line up on the fair ground, each displaying a token of the sort of work being sought. Thus a labourer would wear a smock, a shepherd would carry a crook or wear a wisp of wool in his hat, a thresher an ear of wheat, a carter carried a whip or sported a knot of whipcord. Women and girls in the market would carry a milk-can or butter-pats. After lengthy negotiations, for they were arranging a contract which was binding for the coming year, the farmer would hand over a 'Hiring' or 'fasten' penny, with which the employee would buy a roseatte of ribbon to be worn in his buttonhole.

These mop-fairs endured until well into the twentieth century but were frowned on by moralists who objected to the temptations to which women and girls might be subjected to. But maybe the question, 'O, who will marry me?' sometimes had a ring of desperation about it.

At Horsham in 1844 a woman Nanny Holland was led into the market place with a halter around her neck and sold to a man named Johnson for 30 shillings. The purchaser had to sell his watch to pay for her and for the subsequent celebrations, which involved the consumption of quantities of beer. The sequel is interesting. She lived with Johnson for a year and produced one child. Then she ran away with a man named Jim Smith, whom she married and lived with happily for years!

In about 1820 a woman named Smart was sold at Horsham for 3 shillings and 6 pence. She had been married before and had had two children, and by her new husband she had two more. Then she was put up for sale again and was purchased by a man named Greenfield.

Again at Horsham, in 1825, a journeyman blacksmith offered his wife, by whom he had three children, for sale with a halter around her neck. She was a good-looking woman and was knocked down for £2.5s ... to a purchaser who agreed to take one child. The case was so flagrant, especially the fate of the other two children, that it came to the notice of the local magistrate, who began to make enquiries. But in the meantime the couple had disappeared.

It used to be widely believed that a woman whose husband had died badly in debt took his debts with her when she remarried. Her new husband was therefore responsible but could escape if she would consent to cross the street clad only in her vest. But the matter had to be testified by three male witnesses.

When divorce was prohibited by both Church and State, wife-selling was considered perfectly respectable. Certain formalities had to be observed, however; she had to be sold for at least a shilling and she had to be offered for sale with a halter around her neck. A party of tinkers who, arriving in the village of Swaffham Burbeck in the middle of last century, engaged an auctioneer and publicised a wife sale. Bidding began at sixpence and the woman was finally sold for half-a-crown.

However, a wife sale at Stow, in Suffolk, in 1787 had a rather different result. The price realised was five guineas, which so delighted her first husband that he gave her a guinea to buy a new dress. Then he went over to the church and demanded that the bells be rung to celebrate his concluding so satisfactory a bargain.

The bells of Hatfield Church, in Hertfordshire, were supposed to ring a chime which went;

Lend me your wife today;
I'll lend you mine tomorrow,
No, be like the chimes of Ware,
I'll neither lend nor borrow.

WHEN YOU ARE OLD

When you are old and gray and full of sleep,
And nodding by the fire, take down this book,
And slowly read, and dream of the soft look
Your eyes had once, and of their shadows deep;

How many loved your moments of glad grace,
And loved your beauty with love false or true;
But one man loved the pilgrim soul in you,
And loved the sorrows of your changing face.

And bending down beside the glowing bars
Murmur, a little sadly, how love fled
And paced upon the mountains overhead
And hid his face amid a crowd of stars.

W.B.YEATS (1865-1939)

Hallowe'en is the eve of All Saints' Day (November lst) and is customarily regarded as the first day of winter. It was formerly celebrated by the lighting of bonfires, often on hilltops, and was supposed to mark the date when stores of summer provisions are opened for use in winter.

But it was also reckoned to be one of the days when the boundary between the mundane world and the ethereal world of the spirit became strangely blurred. Those who were so gifted or who took proper precautions could pass at will between the two. It was a date when spirits were abroad, and the wise took steps to propriate them. All sorts of strange things might happen at Hallowe'en. And the seeker after signs and prognostications might expect to be rewarded, though not always in the way he or she would have chosen.

A simple test was for a girl to go to her room at midnight, light a candle, and eat an apple while standing in front of a mirror. Provided she fixes her eyes on her own reflection and does not glance behind her, she will see the phantom of her future sweetheart looking over her shoulder.

Three dishes were arranged on a hearth, before a glowing fire. One dish was empty, one was filled with clean water and one with dirty water. Those who wished to know what the future held for them were blindfolded and, one by one, approached the three bowls and dipped their left hand into one of them. Those who dipped into the empty bowl would never get married; those who found the bowl of clean water would marry the young man or girl of their choice; those who selected the bowl of dirty water would have to be content with a widow or widower.

Great store was set on the behaviour of nuts burning on the hearth, though whether hazel-nuts or chestnuts is not clear. A young couple select their nuts and watch how they burn. If they burn quietly together the omens are good, but if they bounce and pop and jump about the liaison will be stormy.

Where nuts are not available pea-pods will serve. An old rhyme records:

As peapods once I plucked I chanced to see
One that was closely filled with three times three,
Which, when I cropped, I safely home conveyed
And, o'er the door, the spell in secret laid...
The latch moved up, and who should first come in,
But, in his proper person ...

And here is quoted the name of the person desired.

In the North of England when cooking a dish of peas, a housewife will pop in a bean, shell and all. Whoever gets the bean is reckoned to be the first to be married.

Alternatively, if when she retired to bed that night she arranged her shoes by the bedside in the form of the letter 'T' and recited,

Hoping this night my true love to see,
I place my shoes in the form of a 'T'.

she would undoubtedly be rewarded. But, as a matter of fact, what she would be doing was invoking the Scandinavian god, Thor, whose talisman the letter 'T' represents.

In the Scottish Highlands a girl wishing for more information on the character of her young man must go into a field of kale and, with eyes closed, pull the first stalk of kale she comes to. By taking note of its size and straightness she can form some conclusions about him. If any soil sticks to the root, that indicates good fortune.

Or if the couple go into the barn yard and each of them pulls, in turn, three stalks of oats; if the third stalk lacks the 'top-pickle', that is the grain at the top of the stalk, it is a sign that the girl is anything but a virgin!

A portent with all the hallmarks of the supernatural is still known on Scottish croftings involved in dyeing and weaving. The instructions are that you must steal out, entirely alone, to the kiln and throw into the kiln a length of blue yarn. Link it to the yarn already in the kiln and continue winding. As you get towards the end of the yarn something will hold the thread and prevent you from continuing. You then demand, 'Who holds?' And the answer comes from the kiln-pot, consisting of the Christian and surname of your future spouse.

A variation on the business of peeling an apple in front of a mirror is that a girl should take a candle and, standing there alone, should proceed to eat the apple, at the same time combing her hair. The fact of her true love will then be seen, peeping over her shoulder.

Another charm is concerned with the winnowing of corn. Go alone and unperceived to the winnowing barn and open both doors, if possible taking them off their hinges. (The precaution of shutting the doors is to prevent the 'spirit' who is about to appear from doing a mischief, for he is very powerful!) Go through the actions of winnowing corn, and when you repeat them three times the apparition will appear. It will resemble a whirlwind, but will resemble in some respects the figure of your true sweeheart. All very mysterious.

The following, though laconic, is equally spine-chilling. When you are alone go to the rickyard and pace around a barley stack. On the last time round you will become aware, momentarily, of the presence of your true love in your arms.

Go to a south-flowing stream where the domains of three lords meet and dip in it your left shirt-sleeve. Go to bed in front of a fire and hang your wet sleeve before it to dry. Lie awake, and just before midnight an apparition, bearing a distinct resemblance to your sweetheart, will come and turn the sleeve, seeking to dry the other side.

All Souls' day is, of course, the Celtic festival of Samhain, when the year ended and when winter began. Uncanny things happened at Samhain, for ghosts and spirits were free to roam, and the spirits of the dead revisited their earthly haunts. A translation of some lines recorded as occurring on Saint Patrick's breastplate testify to the perils which walked abroad at this season:

God's shield to protect me.
God's legions to save me
from snares of the demons,
from evil enticements,
from failings of nature,
from one man or many
that seek to destroy me
anear or afar.

And, as a modern commentator has put it:

However much the contemporary mind may feel like resisting the traditional Celtic personification

> of such forces, there can be no doubt that malevolent forces operate in our world and through our own spirits and that we need saving from them.

The belief in the returning dead lingered long after the Reformation. To quote Christina Hole (*Traditional English Customs*):

> In Lancashire and Westmorland a farmer would sometimes light a small fire of his own in one of his fields and, when it was burning well and fiercely, would take a mass of flaming straw from it upon a pitchfork and carry it up to the highest point of his land. There he flung it as far as he could over his ground, to purify the soil and guard it against evil, and to make the crops grow in due course. Meantime his family knelt around the bonfire and remembered the dead of their kin. Whether they actually prayed for them or not depended upon their particular form of religion, but there is no doubt that this was the original intention of the custom, and that, prayers or not, the ceremony was believed to help the dead.

In Wales and Scotland there are records of a ceremony in which a white stone is thrown into a roaring bonfire, one for every person present. When the fire dies down a search is made for the stones, and if any are missing it is alleged that the person who contributed it will die within the next twelve months.

Against this bizarre and somewhat sinister background, the association of Hallowe'en with youthful amours does seem rather trivial.

In Somerset Hallowe'en is associated with the celebration on Punkie Night, obviously connected with the festival though held on October 29th. On that evening children and young people (there is even a Punkie Queen) parade in procession around the streets, arrayed in fancy dress and bearing turnip or pumpkin lanterns. As they march they chant:

It's Punkie Night tonight,
It's Punkie Night tonight,
Gie us a candle, gie us a light,
It's Punkie Night tonight.
It's Punkie Night tonight,
Adam and Eve, they wouldn't believe
It's Punkie Night tonight.

Prizes are offered for the most attractive fancy dress. The local villages have concocted a legend to explain the ceremony. They say that it originated when their men folk went to Chiselborough Fair and drank so much cider that they were unable to negotiate a footbridge on the homeward journey. So the women scooped out mangolds which they pulled from a farmer's field, placed lighted candles inside them and proceeded to lead their husbands home.

That the women should find the time for pulling mangolds and carving faces in them (a lengthy procedure) on a dark October night seems an unlikely sequence of events. I toyed with the idea that originally the lanterns were made from pumpkins, though they would seem to be too recent an introduction, but a local resident laughed at me.

No need to invent ideas like that!' she said. 'A Punky is a will-o-the-wisp!'

And so we are brought back again to the supernatural and have to conclude that Punkie Night was, originally, another manifestation of the beliefs connected with Hallowe'en, – of a night when ghosts and spirits might be encountered in the dark lanes of the countryside.

Because I liked you better
  Than suits a man to say,
It irked you, and I promised
  To throw the thought away.

To put the world between us
  We parted, stiff and dry;
'Good-bye', said you, 'forget me.'
  'I will, no fear', said I.

If here, where clover whitens
  The dead man's knoll, you pass,
And no tall flower to meet you
  Starts in the trefolied grass,

Halt by the handsome naming
  The heart no longer stirred,
And say the lad that loved you
  Was one that kept his word.

A.E.HOUSMAN (1859-1936)

The litany of love is strangely lacking at Christmastide. With all the merriment and rejoicing going on, one would have thought there would be ample excuse for matrimonial divinations, but perhaps the general atmosphere of the festival season was so pervasive as to render artificial aids superfluous. After all, we can hardly imagine Christmas without mistletoe and the kissing to which it offers every incentive. An elaboration of this custom is to create a 'kissing bough', on which holly, ivy and mistletoe are fastened to a hooped frame and decorated with oranges, apples and ribbons. Many a young couple doubtless exchanged their first tentative kisses under a 'kissing bough'.

The old custom of the Yule Log is still observed in some country districts, though modern houses have no open hearths on which to burn it. The huge log was dragged into the hall or living-room and lit from an ember from the previous year's log, which had been purposely kept burning all the summer. There was another incentive to keeping the log glowing, for it was supposed to keep the house safe from lightning and fire, as well as bringing good luck. Incidentally, it was considered very unlucky to 'lend' fire, meaning to send embers to a neighbour who had let her own fire go out; if compassion compelled her to relent she had to accept payment for the service.

Divination was an almost compulsory adjunct of first the Christmas pudding, and more recently, the Christmas cake. Every member of the family had traditionally to take a hand with the stirring when the pudding was being made. As they stirred, so they had to wish, and good luck would follow, but on no account must they reveal what they had wished for, or their luck would be reversed. It is now quite customary for the housewife to embed in the mixture, whether for pudding or cake, some small charms, such as a silver coin, a thimble, a ring or an item of jewellery, and the recipients' fortune in what their slice contains. A ring, of course, signifies an approaching marriage, a thimble denotes a life of single blessedness, a coin speaks of coming wealth.

These tokens are also the gifts the 'First-footer' must bring with him as he knocks on the door on the morning of January 1st. He carries with him a slice or loaf of bread, a log, some salt and a little money, and as he hands over these gifts he ensures that the household will have food, warmth and prosperity during the coming year.

Here I would like to insert a description I gave of the 'First-Footer' in a column I write for the *Guardian Weekly*. It incorporates all the information I have about the 'First-footer' and is set in a period two hundred years ago.

> As I strolled down the orchard on New Year's Day a song-thrush, invisible in the mist, was valiantly attempting a few chords of his spring song from a high perch on the old apple-tree. It was the familiar old tree under which my long-deceased great-grandfather used to set up his cider-press, and I peered through the morning gloom to see whether he was there, waiting for a chat. But the figure standing there, looking up into the branches, was not great-grandfather William but great-grandmother Elizabeth.
>
> "Just looking to see if it's still there," she gave as a brief explanation, and I saw she had her gaze fixed on the great besom of mistletoe which has adorned the tree, without apparently ever increasing or diminishing in size, ever since I can remember.
>
> "Yes, and it was here when I was a girl," said

great-grandmother Elizabeth, divining my thoughts. "It brings back happy memories for me."

The big hall of her father's farm, which dated from the time when the house had been a mediaeval manor, was used only on special occasions, but at Christmas it was in service for more than a week.

"After getting it all warmed up for Christmas, it would be a pity to let it grow cold again before the New Year," said her mother.

So big logs, some of which needed two men to carry them, were brought in every few hours to replenish the fire on the hearth, and even then it was chilly in the far corners of the room.

On the last afternoon of the Old Year the hall was the scene of great activity. Furniture was moved to allow space for the big oak table, which was wider than an ordinary trestle table and more than twice as long, to occupy the whole of one side of the hall. Along the other side chairs and benches were arranged, and at either end of the table steps were placed. The stage was set for the annual performance of the Mumming Play.

It is a traditional drama – an allegory of the conflict between light and darkness. Ever since Midsummer the days had been growing shorter and darker, and if the process was not qulckly arrested there would soon be no day at all – only one long night. But now, in the middle of winter, the advance of darkness had been halted, in a ding-dong, rumbustious battle between the champions of darkness and light. There was plenty of action in the play, and lots of blood and a good many fine speeches. At the end the annual miracle had occurred, the stricken hero was restored to life, and from now on light would triumph.

Everybody applauded and then settled down to enjoy the feast, which was soon being conveyed on trays from the kitchen. Mulled cider and punch circulated, along with good and often ribald stories, with interludes of music from the band which had accompanied the play. As the grandfather clock struck twelve the company joined hands and sang 'Auld Lang Syne,' but at the end of the fifth boisterous chorus Elizabeth happened to notice her mother whispering to one of the guests, young William. Soon afterwards William disappeared.

Preparations for departure began, but as coats were being donned and gloves pulled on there came a thunderous knocking at the door.

"Ha! The first-footer!" someone exclaimed.

Elizabeth's father opened the door, and there stood William. In one hand he carried a jar of cider, in the other a loaf of bread, and under his arm a log of wood. The cider and the bread he gave to Elizabeth's father, the log he carried across the room to the fire on the hearth.

"Here's to the New Year!" people called, and someone cried, "Go and make sure the back door's open to let the Old Year out!"

There was silence for a moment, and then great-grandmother Elizabeth spoke.

"Perhaps you've forgotten about that custom," she observed. "William was our first-footer. The first person other than the family to step over the threshold in the New Year must be tall, dark, young and handsome. He mustn't be lame, or have a squint, or have his eyebrows joined in the middle. And he should bring gifts ... bread, cider, a log for the fire. So he brings good luck to the house for the coming year."

Great-grandmother Elizabeth was quiet for a moment.

"My mother was a shrewd woman," she went on. "I didn't think anyone knew I was attracted by William, but evidently she did. She had arranged it all. And afterwards, when he went home and I went with him to the door, he took me in his arms and gave me our first kiss ... under the bunch of mistletoe that hung in the porch! Mistletoe from this same tree. That's why I like to come here to see whether it's still there. It brings back memories ... to me, at any rate. He's forgotten it, I'll be bound!"

"Do you think he has?" came a well-known voice, and we turned to see great-grandfather

William standing behind us. Next second they were in each other's arms, under the mistletoe. I became interested in that thrush, which was still singing overhead, and when I looked down again they were vanishing into the mist. An amorphous shape, gradually dissolving. I couldn't tell whether it was two persons or one.

Shall I compare thee to a summer's day?
Thou art more lovely and more temperate:
Rough winds do shake the darling buds of May,
And summer's lease hath all too short a date:
Sometime too hot the eye of heaven shines,
And often is his gold complexion dimm'd;
And every fair from fair sometime declines,
By chance, or nature's changing course untrimm'd;
But thy eternal summer shall not fade,
Nor lose possession of that fair thou ow'st,
Nor shall death brag thou wander'st in his shade,
When in eternal lines to time thou grow'st,
So long as men can breathe, or eyes can see,
So long lives this, and this gives life to thee.

WILLIAM SHAKESPEARE (1564-1616)

As the years passed, the question assumed an increasing urgency, for in most past ages marriage was the only respectable career for a woman. It is true that a father possessed of a reasonable fortune and with only daughters to inherit it might make ample provision to support them in the single state for the rest of their lives, but such fathers were uncommon and, even then, the unmarried daughter possessed an inferior status to her married sister. She had been 'left on the shelf'.

Fortunately, as is illustrated in the preceding chapter, the girl's mother was fully aware of the problem and did her best to find a solution. And here she had plenty to occupy her.

A girl, and particularly an heiress, must find a suitable husband, which meant a husband in the same class as herself. In the days before the coming of the railways this severely limited the field. The country house families were constantly exchanging visits, but even so the number of marriageable youths and girls was restricted.

What happened is probably illustrated by an incident related to me by a Somerset lady who assured me that it was authentic. It concerns a lady who, dining with the Duke of Wellington, victor of Waterloo, heard the Duke make a derogatory remark about Oliver Cromwell. She immediately sprang to Cromwell's defence.

"Oh no, he was not a bit like that," she declared. "My late husband's first wife's first husband knew him well and had a high opinion of him."

It seems incredible, for Cromwell died in 1658, but we need to take into account the fact that the marriages of heiresses were often based on financial considerations rather than being love matches.

The dinner in question probably took place when the Duke was at the height of his fame, say, in the 1820s. If the lady was then in her eighties she would have been born in the 1740s and so probably married for the first time in the 1760s. Let us assume that her husband was an elderly man who had been young – say, in his twenties – when he married his first wife. That would have been between 1710 and 1720. Again we must assume a heiress, older than he was. If she was then in her forties she would have been born in the 1670s. But she too had been married before, probably in the 1690s, to a man much older than herself. If that first husband of hers had been sixty in the 1690s he could easily have known Oliver Cromwell in the 1650s – and the gap is bridged!

But the marriages in question must have been essentially financial transactions rather than love matches.

Lower in the social scale, the mothers of marriageable girls must have had to exert their influence quite assiduously to entrap a suitable young man from within the limited circle of acquaintances in the group of villages within walking distance. In Victorian times, at least, however, the sons of tradesmen in the nearest town, who were often relations, considerably enlarged the scope. And another source of potential suitors was created by the founding of Nonconformist chapels in the villages, served by local preachers from all parts of the district. Some of these were young and articulate, – just the sort of man to attract a nubile girl.

Nevertheless, the problem loomed increasingly more urgent for the lower classes, – the children of the labouring poor. Though families were large their horizons were incredibly confined. In the village where I grew up in the 1920s, we tended to look for a sweetheart in the group of houses around our home; even the residents living at the other end of the village were more or less 'foreigners'. When the time came for me to marry I chose a girl from my own village, of about 300 inhabitants. We have now lived together for 55 years and look forward to our Diamond Wedding.

The British climate imposes another problem for the course of true love. In May to September, the days are long and the woods and fields offer plenty of places of concealment for courting couples; there are unfortunately few facilities for them in the long, dark months of winter. Barns and hay-sheds were utilised quite extensively by farm workers, but what does a couple do on a long, dark Sunday evening with a storm raging outside? In a cottage with only one living room?

To meet the challenge, the custom of 'bundling' was devised. The young couple were packed off to the bedroom but with the precaution that the girl wore all her clothes and that her ankles and thighs were bound tightly together. Down the middle of the bed was a bolster or wooden plank. The girl lay down on one side of this barrier, the young man on the other. The parents went out and closed the door.

That was bundling in theory, but there were many variations in practice. Imagine a two-roomed cottage on a Sunday evening in winter. It is bedtime, and the younger children have already gone upstairs. The girl and her boy-friend have been sitting by the dying fireside, making desultory conversation and wondering how much longer they had to wait. Eventually the father got up, said good-night and retired.

The mother, before she followed, pulled a bag of oat-chaff from a corner and tossed a bundle of blankets after it. Then the couple was left alone, to do as they pleased. What alternative was there for the parents? They knew well enough what would follow but kept their fingers crossed, in the hope that there would not be an unwanted pregnancy. No doubt the father took a philosophic view of the situation. If Nature took its course and a pregnancy was confirmed, that would mean one mouth the fewer to be fed and one responsibility off his shoulders. In any case, bundling with all the precautions was no guarantee against mishaps. Indeed, there is an alleged record of a father who actually manouevred a young man into a position where he was able to tie him to his daughter until he promised to bundle properly!

In Orkney at Kirkwall Lammas Fair, which was attended by folk from all parts of the island, for the period of the fair a young couple were, if they agreed to be sweethearts, considered honorary brother and sister. They, of course, were allowed all the liberties of a married couple. In Shetland on the occasion of a communal wool-combing the young men and girls who had participated in the day's work laid out a bed of sheaves and spent the night there.

In conclusion, I quote a song recorded by W H Barrett in his *Tales from the Fens*, which he says was a favourite in the taproom of a Cambridgeshire pub:

Now, lasses and lads, hark to my song,
Tis bundle together all the night long;
The game is risky, allow me to say;
One can also get damaged, rolling in hay.

So when the moon is waxing bright,
Across the fen you make for a light
That brightly shines to beckon you on
To the feather bed she lies upon.

You will find the ladder beside the wall,
Out there for the purpose, in case you call.
Raise it quietly, not stopping to linger,
Until, rung by rung, you reach the window.

A gentle tap, and the window's wide open,
And in you go, with no word spoken.
Tread softly, for, the boards may creak,
To awaken the father who's fast asleep.

Nip into bed and snuggle down
Beside the warm body in the nightgown.
But if her sister's there, then rise in a stew
You can bundle with one but not with two.

Now, lusty lads, just listen to me:
A bundle's a bundle, wherever it be.
There's only one ending for me to sing;
The parson won't bless you as he puts on the ring!